HATS

by Dennisha Pratt

Illustrated by Alicia Dianne

HATS

For information regarding permission please contact:
Cue the Bunny LLC at cuethebunny@gmail.com
or
Dennisha Pratt at www.dennishapratt.com

Library of Congress Control Number: 2021914336
ISBN 978-1-7375875-0-7 (Paperback)

This book is dedicated to my family.

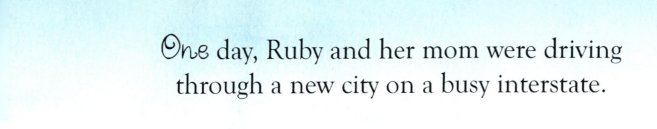

One day, Ruby and her mom were driving
through a new city on a busy interstate.

Ruby knew things were different for her now but couldn't find the words to express it.

She seemed to be lost in her thoughts lately.

"You're going to love this new school!" her mom began to say.

"I remember when I was in elementary school. You'll make new friends in no time!"

Ruby looked out the window
as her mom continued to share.

Suddenly, something caught her attention.

"What was that?" she said to herself.
She looked again.

She saw hats floating and flying in the air.

"How odd," she thought. But where were these lively hats coming from?

The roll-up door on the back of a truck had popped open and sent the hats dancing through the air.

This made Ruby smile.

As she closed her eyes,
she could almost hear...

"THERE'S MY RUBY!!!" She opened her eyes and ran to the source of the voice, waiting with open arms and a huge smile.

"Have I told you how remarkable
you are?" the man said.

"You tell me all the time," said Ruby with a grin. "Well, it's true. Everything down to your hats." Ruby looked with wonder and boldly asked, "Which is your favorite?"

"Good question," he said.

"Your basketball hat always means you're
going to try your best to dunk the ball,
no matter how tall your opponent.

You are a person of incredible grit and passion."

"I love the fancy hats you wear during your ballet recitals. I remember being so proud!

I was impressed with your bravery, as you performed in front of a whole audience."

"When I see your pirate hat, I know we are going on a thrilling adventure.

Your ability to transform any room with the power of your imagination is exceptional."

"A parade is way more fun when you wear your firefighter hat. You always scout out the best places to stand.

Your intuition is admirable.
I have a surprise for you."

He gave Ruby a handmade hat that he'd been working on, just for her. "What would you call this hat?" he asked.

"I'll call it my *conquer the world* hat!"
She declared with a triumphant smile.

"I bet you will," he said with a deep laugh that filled the café. She immediately knew he believed in her.

"Remember, I think the world of you. You are smart, brave, strong, and kind. I love you and I'll always be with you," he said. "I love you too, dad," she said.

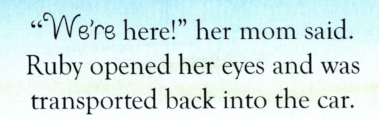

"We're here!" her mom said.
Ruby opened her eyes and was
transported back into the car.

"Are you alright, honey?"

Ruby smiled and said,
"I'm going to be just fine, mom."

Her confident smile grew as she looked toward the clouds above her new school.

"Have a great day, Ruby. Remember I love you."

"I love you too, mom," she replied, as she hopped out of the car with determination.

Boldness rose up in Ruby as she marched forward. She is loved. She is important. She has a purpose in the world. She is never alone. Others have gone ahead of her to pave the way. They are always with her and she can do anything.

Yes, even conquer the world.

Made in the USA
Middletown, DE
26 July 2021